PLAYING with GREAT POWER!

by Sarah Shandera

Plants With Great Power!

tellwell

Tellwell Talent
www.tellwell.ca

ISBN
978-1-77941-636-0 (Paperback)

First Things First:

Always remember
To take a close look,
Name these wild plants
Using a trusted guidebook.

You will find in this book,
Some recipes to try,
But always have an adult help,
To melt, mix and fry.

This will keep us all safe
While we adventure and play,
Filling our minds and our hearts
With new knowledge today.

Come on outside,
Step your feet out the door,
There are treasures to seek,
New worlds to explore!

Grab your favourite hat,
Open your eyes wide to see,
Bring a friend along too,
Come adventure with me!

We will tromp through the forests,
Tiptoe among flowers,
Discover leaves, roots, and berries,
Meet wild plants with great powers!

plantain

(Plantago)

First up on our trek
Is a plant called Plantain.
It grows almost everywhere
There is sunshine and rain.

Wrap the leaf like a band aid,
It soothes and heals most things,
Blisters, cuts, scrapes, and rashes,
And even bee stings.

Fresh Idea: *Fresh plantain can be chewed or crushed, then applied to soothe bites, stings, rashes, scrapes and more!*

Dandelion
(Taraxacum officinale)

Dandelions are special,
So much more than a flower.
Protecting from coughs, colds, and flus,
Is just one secret power.

It helps clear up our skin,
When made into cream,
Try the flowers like fritters,
Or sweet jelly supreme!

Fresh Idea: *The white "milk" found in a fresh dandelion stem can be applied to help get rid of a wart!*

Yarrow

(Achillea millefolium)

Yarrow is amazing!
It stops bleeding, fever and pain.
It can be crushed and applied,
On a wound or a sprain.

So many teeny tiny flowers,
And soft leaves like a fern,
Because Yarrow is so helpful,
It's a plant you should learn.

Fresh Idea: Fresh yarrow leaves can be rolled into a ball and when put into the nose, it can help stop a nosebleed!

Stinging Nettle
(Urtica)

Here's one of my favourite
Power plants that are green,
Stinging nettle might seem scary,
But it's a plant power machine!

Besides keeping our immunity strong,
It can stop bleeding, pain and more,
It helps with digestion,
And when our muscles are sore.

Goldenrod
(solidago)

Goldenrod is a flower
That blooms in late summer and fall.
It's golden yellow in color,
And can grow very tall!

Sore throats and coughs shall be gone,
If you drink Goldenrod tea,
It can relieve pain and swelling,
In joints like your knee.

Pineapple Weed

(Matricaria)

Look very close to the ground,
A weed that is swell,
Pineapple weed is quite common
And gets its name from its smell.

It's related to chamomile,
Like a cousin that's wild,
Makes us feel a bit sleepy,
Calm, peaceful and mild.

chickweed
(Stellaria media)

Take a walk in the garden,
Chickweed is everywhere,
It can really take over,
Make you want to pull out your hair!

But this plant is amazing,
A true superfood,
It's packed so full of nutrition,
It will soon change your mood!

Fresh Idea: Fresh chickweed is a nutritious and delicious snack that tastes like pea sprouts!

So now you have met
Some plants with great power,
All stored deep within
Leaves, seeds, roots, and flower.

These plants all grow wild
You've learned just a few,
Perhaps you can find them
In the world around you.

There are more plants to explore,
Waiting to help us along,
To give us a boost,
Making us happy, healthy, and strong.

Recipes to Try

Plantain Salve (First Aid Ointment)

Apply to burns, rashes, bug bites and stings, hives, cuts, and scratches.

Ingredients:

- 1\2 cup dried plantain leaves. Pick fresh leaves from a clean area and hang them in a cloth bag in your window or use a dehydrator.
- 1\2 cup olive oil
- 2 Tbsp beeswax
- 10 drops tea tree oil (optional as an antiseptic and preservative)

Instructions:

1. Crush dried leaves with your fingers and put them in a container or jar with the olive oil. Allow to sit for a week or longer, shaking the jar daily to move around the leaves.
2. When the oil is ready, strain the leaves out through a tight mesh strainer

3. Melt beeswax in a double boiler or in a small jar that is sitting in boiling water. Watch closely!
4. When the wax is melted, stir in the infused oil. The wax may harden slightly as the cool oil is added but keep stirring until they are completely mixed.
5. Remove from heat and add the tea tree oil if using, stir completely.
6. Pour the oil/wax mixture into a tin or small jar and allow it to cool. The salve will harden as it cools and is ready to use once it hardens.

Dandelion Fritters

These are delicious springtime snacks to serve alongside any meal, a bowl of ice cream or on their own! Be sure to choose flowers from an area that has not been sprayed or visited by pets!

Ingredients:

- 4 cups freshly picked and washed dandelion flowers.
- 2 cups flour
- 2 eggs
- 2 cups milk
- Salt 1tsp or to taste
- Honey, maple syrup or icing sugar

Instructions:

1. Mix flour, eggs, milk, salt and other spices if using in a bowl.
2. Heat 1 inch of olive oil in a skillet. Keep it over medium/high heat.

3. Holding the flower side down, dip the dandelion into the batter and swirl around until completely coated.
4. Place the battered dandelion flower side down into the skillet of oil.
5. Remove with a slotted spoon onto a paper towel covered plate.

Goldenrod Tea

Goldenrod is packed full of Vitamin C, and antioxidants. It is delicious hot or cold as an iced tea. Sweeten with honey for a delicious nourishing tea. Goldenrod tea will help soothe sore throats, boost immunity, and help flush out the urinary system.

- **Please be sure of your identification of any plant before ingesting.**
- Remember to source your goldenrod from an area that has not been sprayed or visited by pets!

Ingredients:

- Fresh or dried goldenrod leaves and young flowers (rinsed) (1 very generous tsp per cup of water)
- Fresh boiled water
- Raw honey to taste

Instructions:

1. Place freshly rinsed leaves and young flowers into a tea ball or mesh tea bag.
2. Pour hot water over the bag and allow the tea to steep for 10 min.
3. Sweeten as desired with honey.

Chickweed Pesto

This is a delicious and refreshing pesto to eat with crackers or pita, on a burger, tossed in pasta or on a pizza! Chickweed is a superfood that is packed with nutritious green goodness.

Ingredients:

- 3 cups fresh chickweed
- 3 cloves garlic
- 1\2 cup olive oil
- Juice from one lemon
- 1\2 cup walnuts

Instructions:

1. Place all ingredients except the oil into a food processor
2. Process on high until pureed but still a bit chunky.
3. Slowly add the oil
4. Add salt and pepper to taste

About the Author

Sarah Shandera is a homeschooling mom who lives in rural Alberta with her herbalist husband and their six children. Sarah grew up immersed in plant and animal life. She can be found most days hanging out with her honeybees, or adventuring with friends and family, marvelling over birds, plants, and mushrooms. This is Sarah's first book and represents her love for art, the natural world, and a good read.

Printed in the USA
CPSIA information can be obtained
at www.ICGtesting.com
LVHW060038050324
773408LV00001B/3
* 9 7 8 1 7 7 9 4 1 6 3 6 0 *